© 2006 Hallmark Licensing, Inc.

Published by Gift Books from Hallmark,
a division of Hallmark Cards, Inc.,
Kansas City, MO 64141
Visit us on the Web at www.Hallmark.com

Editorial Director: Todd Hafer
Editor: Jeff Morgan
Art Director: Kevin Swanson
Designer: Mary Eakin
Production Artist: Dan Horton

BOK4324
Printed in China

ISBN: 978-1-59530-144-4

GRANDPARENTS

at the heart of it all

GIFT BOOKS
from Hallmark

GRANDPARENTS

at the heart of it all

SOMETIMES THERE'S NO FRIEND

*in the whole world who's
as much a friend as a grandparent.*

GRANDPARENTS HAVE A WONDERFUL WAY

of giving, of helping, and especially of loving.

EVERY TIME THEY COME TO MIND,

they bring happiness with them.

———

THEY SHARE SO MUCH...

so gladly and so often.

———

THEY CAN BE TEACHERS,
guides, inspirations, examples.

THEY KNOW THE RIGHT BALANCE

between gentleness and strength,
patience and action, responsibility and fun.

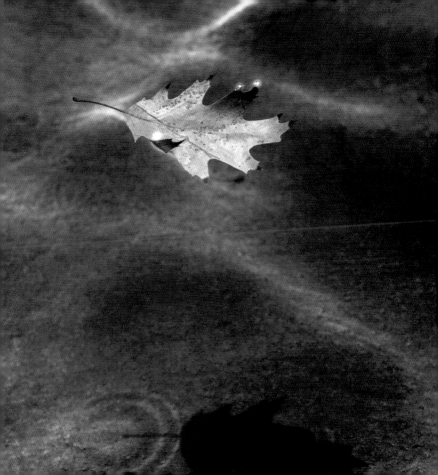

THE BEST GRANDMAS AND GRANDPAS

are kind and supportive,
full of life, laughter, and deep-down love.

———

THEY ARE AT THE CENTER
of so much happiness,
so many family memories.

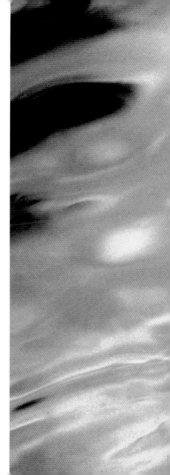

FOR ALL THE THINGS THEY HAVE DONE
and continue to do for their families,
grandparents are admired, respected, and loved.

THEIR WORDS ARE KIND.
Their ways are caring.
Their influence is welcome
and warmly received.

A GRANDMA OR A GRANDPA

has the most open arms
a grandchild could ever run to.

AND, SOMEHOW, THEY ALWAYS SEEM
*to have enough time when it comes
to being with their family.*

THOUGHTS OF THEM ALWAYS
bring some of life's
most special moments to mind.

THEIR FAMILY'S LIFE IS RICHER
*for every tradition they've preserved
and every memory they've shared.*

THEY ARE ALWAYS THERE FOR US,
even across many miles,
caring and giving in the ways
that matter most.

GRANDPARENTS SUPPORT US THROUGH HARD TIMES,
encourage us through stubborn times,
and love us through all times.

THEIR LOVE BRIGHTENS THE WHOLE WORLD...

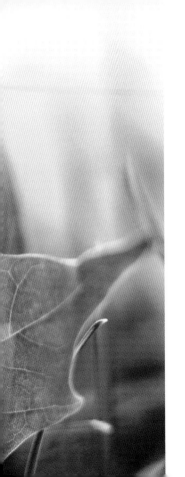

THEY HAVE SUNSHINE

in their smiles.

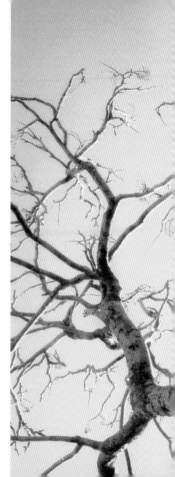

AND THEY ARE THE WARMEST
and brightest lights
on our family tree.

SPECIAL TIMES SHARED WITH THEM

become permanent memories.

OF ALL THE THINGS
a grandma or a grandpa shares,
the very best is love.

AND WHILE THEY ARE ALWAYS REMEMBERED
for their warm words and kind deeds,
they are especially remembered
for that wonderful, unconditional love.

═══

THEY TOUCH SO MANY LIVES

in so many ways.

YOUNG GRANDCHILDREN SEE THEIR GRANDPARENTS
as infallible heroes and heroines.
Adult grandchildren see them as
people of strength and understanding.

———

THEIR LOVE ENCIRCLES THEIR FAMILY

and keeps it close.

THROUGH THEM,

we receive our heritage.
Through them,
we understand the past.
Through them,
we discover who we are.

———

THEIR YEARS OF GIVING AND LOVING

create generations of joy and gratitude.

OFTEN THEY ARE AT THE HEART OF,

the most important part of,

moments too important to forget.

———————

GRANDMA AND GRANDPA
*are different words
for warmth, caring,
and acceptance.*

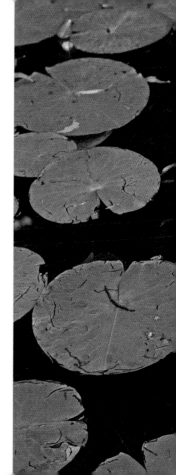

WHEN GRANDPARENTS ARE PRESENT,

the family is always in good company.

———

THEY ARE A CRUCIAL PART

of all we will ever be.

THEY SHARE THE BENEFITS

of their experiences.

FROM GENERATION TO GENERATION

they pass on a legacy of love.

IT IS A CLOSENESS THAT REACHES

across miles and years.

HOW CAN SOMETHING AS TENDER AND GENTLE
as that love be so strong, so sturdy,
and so enduring?

———

THERE'S A PLACE WHERE WE ALWAYS

feel welcome to be ourselves.
That place is anywhere with our grandparents...

———

BECAUSE THEY ARE ALWAYS RIGHT THERE,
at the heart of the family,
with the best stories, the greatest smiles,
and the biggest hearts ever.

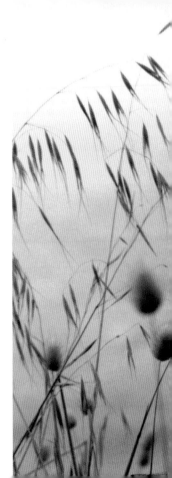

THEIR HOME IS A PLACE
*of warmth and welcome
filled with their presence,
making their family feel
completely at ease.*

TO BE WITH A GRANDMA OR GRANDPA

is to be in loving hands.

THEY HAVE A KNOWLEDGE OF LIFE AND LOVE

not found in books, but in the heart.

THEIR HISTORIES AND LIFE EXPERIENCES

*give meaning to all our todays
and confidence to all our tomorrows.*

––––––––

THEIR REWARD IS TO HAVE AS MANY REASONS

to be happy as their family has reasons

for loving them.

═══

IN SOME OF OUR MOST
memorable family occasions,
we find the loving presence of grandparents.

SO MANY SPECIAL MOMENTS
shared with them
flow into love-filled years.

GRANDMAS AND GRANDPAS TEACH US
*that each new stage of life
brings new interests, new dreams,
and new possibilities.*

THEY ARE A WONDERFUL MIXTURE

of gentleness and strength,
wisdom and understanding,
warmth and love.

THEY ADD SO MANY MEANINGFUL PAGES

to our albums of memories.

THEY ARE PEOPLE TO THINK ABOUT OFTEN...

and hold close always.

A GRANDPARENT IS
a special friend,
never far from thought,
ever near in love.